Go Be Amazing!

By
Amy Miller

Dedication

This book is dedicated to my AMAZING dad and mom. They taught me that I didn't have to be THE best, but I should always be MY best. They have always encouraged, cheered, and pushed my sister and me to be the very best versions of ourselves. We were truly blessed to be raised in home of love, compassion, and grace; a home that we were expected to give all of ourselves to whatever we did.

My husband and I have raised two beautiful daughters that we have spilled this into. For as along I can remember I would send them off to school or wherever they were going with a "Go Be Amazing"!

This carried over into my classroom as I end each day with the very same words. They are simply a reminder to my "kids" to go into the world being the very best they can be!

SCHOOL TIMETABLE

Monday						
Tuesday						
Wednesday						
Thursday						
Friday						

Helping at home, this is amazing too. Even the tiniest of humans, there is so much you can do.